ALL-COLOUR VEGETARIAN RECIPES

Edited by Christopher & Jean Conil

W. Foulsham & Co. Ltd.
London • New York • Toronto •
Cape Town • Sydney

1

W. Foulsham & Company
Limited
Yeovil Road, Slough,
Berkshire, SL1 4JH

ISBN 0-572-01715-4

Originally published
by Falken-Verlag
GmbH, Niedernhausen/TS
West Germany.
Photographs copyright
© 1985 Falken-Verlag
This English language
edition copyright
© 1992 W. Foulsham
& Co. Ltd.

Printed in Hong Kong.

2

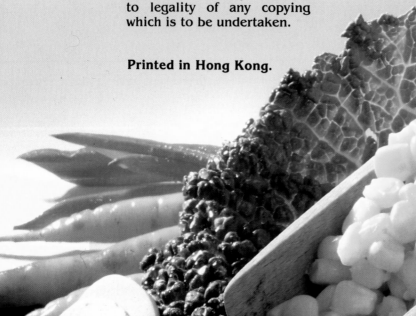

Contents

Introduction

Nutrients

We distinguish between nutrients which yield energy (proteins, fats and carbohydrates) and those which yield no energy (vitamins, minerals, fibre and water). The amount of nutients required by an individual depends on many factors — environmental influences, age, race, body build, work and leisure activities, to name just a few. Some nutrients are described as vital; in other words they are absolutely necessary for the human body. These substances must be given to the body regularly in the form of food, since unbalanced nutrition deprives the body of important 'building bricks', resulting in deficiency diseases. We should try, therefore, to make our weekly menu as varied as possible, but at the same time restricting our total intake as much of the surplus food we eat is stored as fat, and is detrimental to our health.

Protein

Protein is a vital nutrient which the body must have in correct quantities. Its function is to build up and maintain the muscles and inner organs. Without protein, a child's body will not grow, nor will its cells be renewed. It is also important to consume the right type of protein to ensure a sufficient intake of the eight essential amino acids.

The amount of protein required differs from person to person according to age, build and the type of work done. An adult should take in about 0.8g (0.03 oz) of protein per kg (2.2 lb) of body weight. Not every sort of protein is of equal value, however; this variation is called the biological balance of protein. The more similar the food protein is to body protein, the more valuable it is, as the body needs to consume less to achieve the required amount.

The calorific value of 1g (0.04 oz) protein amounts to 4.1 kcal (kilocalories) or 17kJ (kilojoule). Only ovo-lacto vegetarians and lacto-vegetarians can achieve their required intake of protein with eggs, milk and dairy products. Strict vegetarians must supply their bodies with protein through combinations of diverse foods — for instance, the soya bean as all soya bean products yield biologically valuable protein. Vegans of course do not eat eggs or dairy animal products, making it vital for them to find alternative sources of protein.

Fat

Fat plays an important role in nutrition, although the steep increase in the number of overweight people in the Western World is partly due to over-consumption of fat.

Fat should not simply be condemned, however, because it is also an important nutrient and contains the fat-soluble vitamins A and E. So some fat must be included in the diet, but it should be incorporated into our menus with care: 1g (0.04 oz) fat yields 9.3 kcal or 38kJ.

Generally, fats are described as being animal or vegetable or, according to their consistency, as hard, soft or liquid. The melting point of a certain kind of fat influences its digestibility; the closer the melting point is to the body temperature, the easier the fat is to digest. All fats are composed of glycerine and various fatty acids which are again divided into saturated, unsaturated and polyunsaturated. Saturated, or animal fats, contain cholesterol which is needed for building up hormones and gall liquid. Too much cholesterol in the blood can lead to arteriosclerosis and heart disease and should therefore be kept to a minimum, so we are now advised to use unsaturated, or vegetable fats, rather than saturated fats. Linseed, sunflower, soya and corn oil are particularly recommended.

Carbohydrates

Carbohydrates consist of carbon, hydrogen and oxygen and are vital for providing energy: 1g (0.04 oz) carbohydrates yields 4.1kcal or 17kJ.

Carbohydrates can be divided into primary sugar (glucose, fructose, etc.), sucrose (from cane and beet), lactose (from milk) and maltose (from starch, cellulose and pectin).

Starch is of special importance in our diet. Carbohydrates occur in rice, cereals, corn, potatoes and other roots such as yams, fruit and vegetables. Refined crystallized sugar is a 'no-go' in terms of conscious good nutrition — it is responsible among other things for caries and obesity in many people. The body transforms unused carbohydrates into fat and stores it in fat deposits within the body.

Minerals

Minerals are inorganic substances, some of which are vital for the human body. These essential minerals are needed for the metabolism, but they also influence the functioning of the nerves. Apart from that they fulfil special tasks such as building the bones, parts of the teeth, hormones and enzymes. A well-balanced diet will provide sufficient minerals.

Some minerals appear in greater amounts in our bodies, for instance potash, sodium, magnesium, phosphorus, calcium, chloride, and sulphur. Others appear only in minute traces within our bodies; the most important of these are iodine, iron, cobalt, copper, manganese and zinc. Their main task is to catalyze enzymes into action, transport nutrients and build up blood and hormones.

Even today, we are uncertain about the importance of many minerals. Some of them are even toxic in large quantities.

Vitamins

Vitamins are vital for human beings. As the body is incapable of building up these substances itself from other foodstuffs, they must be taken in with food. Vitamins provide no energy, but they are essential for directing and regulating the metabolism. If the intake of vitamins is too low, deficiency diseases will appear. We distinguish between water soluble vitamins (B and C) and fat soluble vitamins (A, D, E and K).

The vitamin content of food can be influenced by the way the dishes are prepared.

In uncooked, untreated food it is highest; therefore fruit and vegetables should be eaten raw or cooked very quickly in only a little water. With cereal dishes, the whole grains with bran should be used wherever possible. Milk and dairy products are important for providing us with vitamins, but try to avoid tinned and ready-made products. Low-fat milk and yoghurt or buttermilk whey are highly recommended.

Fibre

Fibre is the cellulose or plant fibre which we cannot digest and must, therefore, excrete. Fibre swells in the intestines and provides the food base for intestinal micro-organisms, making it vital for healthy, regular digestion. It is found in all kinds of corn, vegetables, salad stuff, fruit and potatoes, but also in wheatgerm and linseed. Our new healthy eating habits have changed drastically in recent years with the Nouvelle Cuisine both accepting and promoting the use of raw vegetables and fruit either as a garnish or complimentary food item. Eating more raw vegetables is recommended for many ailments and eases the process of digestion, hence improving our health generally.

Water

The human body consists of 60–70 percent of water. Because the body loses water constantly it must be replaced in sufficient amounts. One can survive for a longer period of time without food, but without water, the whole metabolism soon comes to a halt.

Water transports substances in our body, but it also serves as a medium for bathing the body organs and keeps the body temperature even. The amount of water a body needs depends on many factors — 35g (1.2 oz) per kg (2.2 lb) of body weight is a guideline. This means 2–2.5 litres/3½–4½ pints daily for the average adult. When drinking water, distilled, spring or mineral water are preferable.

Points to Remember When Shopping

In our modern world, shopping has become relatively easy. Health-food shops, supermarkets or delicatessens are within easy reach of most of us, and these have everything required for vegetarian cooking. You will probably be surprised at the diversity and high quality of the foods on display there. For your information, we have listed the most important products, and a few useful hints. One further tip is to shop frequently for fresh foods. Wilted vegetables, for example, have lost much of their food value.

Drinking-Whey

Drinking-whey is an excellent drink which is also extremely healthy. It consists of milk liquid, minerals, water-soluble milk vitamins, lactic sugar and lactic acid. Drinking-whey is available in various different flavours, either as natural whey or with added fruit. It tastes best when cool. Whey powder can also be used to make a delicious, healthy drink as can buttermilk either as it is or diluted with soda water.

Biogarde

This yoghurt is made from special cultures of milk bacteria in which there is a large quantity of right turning lactic acid which is especially easy for the human body to digest. Quark, quark products and cottage cheese are made in a similar way and are all widely available in shops or simple to make at home. Natural quark is a curd cheese made by the coagulation or curdling of milk casein by lemon juice or a similar acidic agent. Lemon juice produces a soft curd, while vinegar produces a harder, coarser curd.

Milk and Dairy Products

For lacto-vegetarians it is very important to eat the right dairy products. Of course, it's best if you can get milk from a local farmer who rears his cows on organic foodstuffs. Otherwise, you must look for dairy products from organically reared animals, especially goats, in health food shops in order to ensure that the products are free from chemical additives.

Wholewheat Flour

Try to replace white flour and products made from white flour with wholewheat flour as often as possible, as it provides important vitamins and fibre. Be sure that all the wholewheat you buy is grown organically and that it is freshly ground. For fancy pastries, use very finely ground flour. The bran left over after sieving can be used in other dishes, for instance stuffing or soups. Freshly ground flour should be used relatively quickly, since it soon goes rancid and loses all its nutrients.

Soya Products

Apart from soya beans, health-food shops offer a wide variety of soya products. Soya provides high-quality protein and is better than meat or animal protein. With a little imagination, you can make dishes from soya that are very similar to meat dishes and which may influence even the most dedicated opponents of vegetarianism. There are also plenty of ready-made products like goulash, rissoles and spreads which likewise are very tasty.

Tofu is the best soya product. This is soya cheese which is made from ripe, soaked, then cooked soya beans to which are added gelling agents. This mixture is pressed into convenient shapes, without added preservatives, and then packed. In eastern Asia, Tofu has been one of the most important protein sources for more than 2000 years. (See *The Secret of Tofu* by Christopher and Jean Conil, Foulsham.)

Tofu has a more or less bland taste, will accept any flavouring and, due to its texture, can be grilled, baked, fried, steamed or stir-fried Chinese style.

Soya milk is healthier than cow's milk and can replace it in cooking. Soya sauce is produced by fermentation and is used as a flavouring in much modern cookery. Worcester sauce is produced from soya sauce.

Soya flour is the dehydrated form of soya bean. It can replace eggs in many recipes and enrich starchy products with additional protein nutrients.

Oils and Fat

When using oil you should buy only oils made from one fruit, i.e. olive oil, sunflower, soya, peanut or walnut oil, etc. There are several ways of producing oil, but you should choose oil from cold pressings. It is somewhat more expensive but tastes better and is very high in nutrients. This oil is made from fresh, ripe fruit.

Although the choice of butter or vegetable margarine is individual, vegetable margarine contains unsaturated fats and are therefore lower in cholesterol. It is best used in purées, cakes or puddings. For roasting or grilling, food can be lightly brushed with vegetable oil. Deep-fried foods should be avoided wherever possible.

Vinegar

Not all vinegars are the same. In Britain, people prefer malt vinegar, whereas Mediterranean countries tend to use wine vinegar. The Americans prefer cider vinegar because malic acid is less corrosive than the acetic acid in other vinegars. Which kind of vinegar you decide on is a matter of taste, but we would recommend cider vinegar, since it is more wholesome. It is the acidity content which distinguishes the various kinds of vinegar, therefore try a particular type before using it in salads, etc. to ensure the taste is not too acidic for you. The acidity is generally stated on the label

— normal vinegar contains 5 per cent vinegar acid.

You can also enhance your vinegar by adding fruit or herbs. For 1 litre (1.8 pints) of vinegar you will need about 200–300g (7–11 oz) of fruit or 50–100g (2–4 oz) herbs. Transfer the vinegar and herbs to a jar, close the lid well and leave to 'set' for a fortnight, shaking the jar occasionally. Then strain and transfer to a clean bottle ready for use.

Sugar

Sugar should be avoided as much as possible as it makes fat deposits in the body if it is not utilised as energy and can also cause damage to the teeth. Honey consists of glucose, a sweetener which is absorbed into the blood-stream more quickly than sucrose and is therefore a good alternative to other sugars. In Britain, Sweetex liquid or crystals is a great help in reducing sugar intake.

Seasoning Agents

Extracts from vegetable stock or yeast stock are very good for adding flavour, as are spice mixtures and herb salts. Try several — you are sure to find something to your liking. Fresh herbs and spices are best of all.

Brewer's Yeast

Brewer's yeast can provide B vitamins, minerals and protein and serves as an excellent seasoning agent. Brewer's yeast is available as powder, tablets or in a paste form like Marmite or soya paste (miso).

Salt

Salt is one of our basic spices, and a vital part of healthy nutrition. However, too much salt is unhealthy. Salt is divided into cooking salt, table salt, sea salt and various herb salts. Salt is a welcome addition to many dishes, but should be used very sparingly. For vegetarian cooking one should use sea salt or potassium chloride.

Dinner Parties for Every Occasion

Birthday Dinner

Medley of Vegetable Fritters
Wild Herb Soup
Tofu Ragout
Chocolate Cherry Slice

Beer Dinner

Herbed Vegetable Rice
Beetroot and Tofu Soup
Boiled Potatoes with Dips
Semolina Slices with
Raspberry Sauce

Wine Dinner

Celeriac Salad
Mushroom Crescents
Asparagus in White Wine
Sauce
Mixed Fruit Salad with Nuts

Hearty Dinner

Betroot and Tangerine Salad
Sweet and Sour Spinach
Ravioli
Brittany Soup
Italian Cheese Pickle and
Herbed Oat Bread

Italian Dinner

Ratatouille Pie with Cheese
Sauce
Tomato Angelo
Lasagne al Forno
Apricot Tart with Coconut

Chinese Dinner

Peking Soup
Baked Honey Beans
Savoury Choux Fritters
Home-made Almond Ice
Cream

Gourmet Dinner

Tomato Angelo
Spring Vegetable Soup
Quiche Lorraine
Apricot Tart with Coconut

Quick Dinner

Carrot and Orange Salad
Vegetableburgers
Madrid Salad
Rolled Oats with Cherry
Cream

Sunday Dinner

Love Apple Soup
Hungarian Soya Goulash
Baked Potatoes in Soured
Cream Gratin
Fruit Pizza

Light Dinner

Baked Apple Stuffed with
Walnuts
Chinese Egg and Mushroom
Soup
Celeriac Salad
Tutti-Frutti Jelly

Diet Dinner

Tropical Fruit Cocktail
Delicious Carrot Soup
Cabbage and Rice Roulade
Apple Sorbet with Mint

9

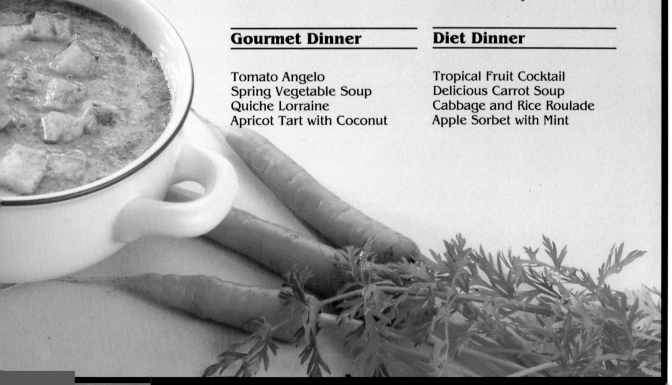

Italian Cheese Pickle

Ingredients	Metric/Imperial
Olive oil	225ml/8fl oz
Chillies, seeded and sliced	2/2
Garlic cloves, chopped	2–4/2–4
Black peppercorns	15ml/1 tbsp
Juniper berries	4/4
Bay leaf	1/1
Rosemary or basil	1sprig/1sprig
Thyme	1 sprig/1 sprig
Spanish onion	1 medium/1 medium
Provolone cheese	100g/4oz
Bel Paese cheese	100g/4oz
Gorgonzola cheese	100g/4oz
Mozzarella cheese	100g/4oz

Slice the onion, cut the cheese into bite-size pieces without any loose crumbs and arrange in a jar. Add the chillies, garlic, herbs and spices.

Pour the oil on top and leave to marinate in the fridge for at least 12 hours.

Drain the cheese and serve with Herbed Oat Bread.

10

Herbed Oat Bread

Ingredients	Metric/Imperial
Rolled oats	100 g/4 oz
Buttermilk	150–200 ml/5–7 fl oz
Wholewheat flour	250g/9oz
Dried yeast	10g/1 tsp
Butter	30ml/2 tbsp
Sea salt	a pinch/a pinch
Chives, snipped	15ml/1 tbsp
Parsley, chopped	15ml/1 tbsp
Marjoram, chopped	15ml/1 tbsp
Caraway seeds	5ml/1 tsp

Additionally:

Egg yolks, beaten	2/2
Aniseed	15ml/1 tbsp
Cardamom pods	5ml/1 tsp
Caraway seeds	5ml/1 tsp

Grind two-thirds of the oats in a blender or grinder. Mix with the buttermilk and leave to stand for 2 hours. Combine the yeast with 5ml/1tsp flour and 45ml/3tbsp tepid water. Leave for 10 minutes to activate. Combine the flour and yeast mixture with the ground oats,

the remaining oats, the butter, salt, chopped herbs, and caraway seeds. Mix to make a compact dough. Leave to rise, covered, in a warm place for 30–40 minutes.

Knead the dough well, then divide into three equal parts.

Sprinkle a worktop with flour and roll out into three strands, then plait into a braid.

Place on a floured baking sheet, cover and leave to rise for 30 minutes. Bake in an oven preheated to 220°C/425°F/Gas 7 for 30 minutes.

Mix the yolks with a little water. Shortly before the bread is cooked, brush it with the yolks and sprinkle with aniseed, caraway seeds and crushed or ground cardamom.

Remove from the oven, cool and serve with the Italian Cheese Pickle.

Tip

Aniseed can be replaced with either poppy or sesame seeds.

Sweet and Sour Spinach Ravioli

Ingredients   Metric/Imperial

For the pastry:

Finely ground wholewheat flour	400g/14oz
Eggs, beaten	4/4
Sea salt	5g/1 tsp
Olive oil	15–30 ml/1–2 tbsp
Milk	30ml/2 tbsp
Eggs, separated	2/2
Fresh spinach, cooked or frozen spinach, thawed	450 g/1 lb
Onion, chopped	1 medium/1 medium
Breadcrumbs	45–60 g/3–4 tbsp

Sea salt to taste
Freshly ground black pepper to taste

For the sauce:

Onions, chopped	2/2
Chives, snipped	30ml/2 tbsp
Parsley, chopped	15ml/1 tbsp
Tarragon, chopped	15ml/1 tbsp
Hard-boiled (Hard-cooked) eggs	2/2
Cider vinegar	30ml/2 tbsp
Vegetable stock	225ml/8 fl oz
Olive oil	30ml/2 tbsp
Mustard	15ml/1 tbsp
Lemon	1/2/1/2
Orange marmalade	15 ml/1 tbsp

Sieve the flour on to a large wooden board and make a well in the centre. Add the eggs and combine with the salt and oil to make a smooth pastry. Add some milk if necessary. Cover and leave to stand in a warm place for at least 30 minutes. Roll out thinly on a floured worktop, cover again and leave to stand for 15 minutes.

In the meantime, separate the eggs and combine the yolks with the spinach, onion, breadcrumbs, salt and pepper.

Cut the pastry into small squares, and cover half of them with spinach. Brush the edges with lightly whisked egg white, then cover with the remaining squares. Be sure to press the edges firmly together.

Boil the filled pasta in salted water for 10–15 minutes, remove, drain well and keep warm.

To make the sauce, combine the chopped eggs with the herbs and onion. Pour the vinegar, stock, oil, mustard, lemon juice and marmalade on top, mix well then season to taste with salt and pepper.

Arrange the spinach pasta on plates, pour the sauce on top and serve.

Ratatouille Pie with Cheese Sauce

Ingredients	Metric/Imperial
Butter or margarine	45ml/3 tbsp
Spanish onion	1 medium/1 medium
Courgette (Zucchini)	1/1
Cucumber	1 small/1 small
Beef (steak) tomatoes, peeled and seeded	2 large/2 large
Aubergine (Eggplant)	1/1
Sea salt to taste	
Oregano, chopped	30ml/2 tbsp
Chives, snipped	30ml/2 tbsp
Freshly ground black pepper to taste	

For the sauce:

Butter or margarine	45ml/3 tbsp
Wholewheat flour	45–60 ml/3–4 tbsp
Milk	½l/18 fl oz
Ground nutmeg	a pinch/a pinch
Grated Parmesan cheese	50g/2oz

Additionally:

Mozzarella cheese	125 g/4½ oz

Grease an ovenproof dish. Slice the onion, courgette, cucumber and tomatoes. Slice the aubergine and sprinkle with salt. Leave for 30 minutes then rinse and pat dry.

Arrange the vegetables in layers in the dish. Sprinkle each layer with herbs, salt and pepper.

For the sauce, heat the butter or margarine in a pan and stir in the flour. Add the milk, stirring constantly. Bring the sauce to the boil and stir until it is smooth and creamy. Season with the salt, pepper and nutmeg.

Pour the sauce over the vegetables, then cover with the sliced Mozzarella. Sprinkle with Parmesan.

Bake for 20–30 minutes in an oven preheated to 200°C/400°F/Gas 6. Remove and serve immediately.

. . . .

Tip

You can of course use other vegetables for this dish, for instance cauliflower and broccoli. Firm vegetables should, however, be parboiled before baking.

. . . .

Mushroom Turnovers

Ingredients   Metric/Imperial

Frozen puff pastry	450g/1lb

For the stuffing:

Butter or margarine	30ml/2 tbsp
Onion, chopped	1 medium/1 medium
Mushrooms, sliced	350g/12oz
Chives, snipped	15ml/1 tbsp
Parsley, chopped	15ml/1 tbsp
Watercress, chopped	1 bunch/1 bunch
Eggs	3/3
Sea salt to taste	
Freshly ground pepper to taste	
Nutmeg, ground	a pinch/a pinch

Additionally:

Egg yolk	1/1
Grated Parmesan cheese	50g/2oz

Roll out the defrosted pastry on a floured worktop.

Heat the butter or margarine in a pan and gently sauté the onion until translucent. Add the mushrooms and fry for 1-2 minutes. Stir in the herbs.

Beat the eggs, season with salt, pepper and nutmeg. Pour over the mushrooms and cook until set, stirring constantly. Remove from the heat and leave to cool.

Spread the mushroom mixture on the pastry, fold over and firmly press the edges together. Place on to a

baking tray sprinkled with water and bake for 20 minutes in an oven preheated to 200°C/400°F/Gas 6.

Shortly before the time

up, brush the pastry with the egg yolk, combined with a little water, and sprinkle with Parmesan.

Remove and serve either hot or cold.

Tip

Any type of fresh or dried mushrooms available can be used for this dish. Delicatessens, health-food shops and supermarkets stock a wide range, although some do tend to be expensive.

Phyllo pastry can be used instead of puff pastry and does not have to be defrosted or rolled. It should be handled carefully, however, as it is very thin and tears easily.

Delicious Carrot Soup

Ingredients	Metric/Imperial
Carrots	600g/1 ½ lb
Butter or margarine	45 ml/3 tbsp
Vegetable stock	600 ml/1 pt
Sea salt to taste	
Freshly ground pepper to taste	
Sugar	a pinch/a pinch
Chervil, chopped	30 ml/2 tbsp
Sparkling wine	30 ml/2 tbsp
Single cream (Light cream)	100 ml/4 fl oz

Peel the carrots and cut them into small pieces, then fry gently in butter or margarine until translucent.

Pour in the stock, bring to the boil and cook for 30 minutes. Cool then purée in a food processor. Return the soup to the pan, reheat and season to taste with salt, pepper and sugar.

Stir in the chervil, then add a splash of sparkling wine. Remove from the heat and fold in the cream.

Pour into individual bowls and serve immediately.

Tip

You can replace the carrots with pumpkin to make this exquisite soup.

Wild Herb Soup

Ingredients	Metric/Imperial
Spinach	250g/9oz
Young stinging nettles	100g/4oz
Sorrel	50g/2oz
Lettuce	1 medium/1 medium
Butter or margarine	30 ml/2 tbsp
Onion, chopped	1/1
Vegetable stock	400 ml/14 fl oz
Sea salt to taste	
Freshly ground pepper to taste	
Nutmeg	a pinch/a pinch
Single cream (Light cream)	100 ml/4 fl oz
Egg yolks, beaten	4/4

Additionally:

Wholewheat bread	4 slices/4 slices
Butter or margarine	60 ml/4 tbsp

Wash the spinach, stinging nettles, sorrel and lettuce thoroughly, then chop finely.

Heat the butter or margarine in a pan and gently fry the chopped onion until translucent. Add the vegetables, then pour in the stock. Bring to the boil and simmer for 15 minutes. Season with salt, pepper and nutmeg. Cool slightly and purée in a food processor. Return to the pan and reheat.

Whisk the cream with the yolks until smooth. Remove the soup from the heat and stir in the cream.

Cut the bread into small cubes, toast in the butter or margarine until golden brown, sprinkle on top of the soup and serve.

Chunky Vegetable Soup

Ingredients	Metric/Imperial
Butter or margarine	60 ml/4 tbsp
Spring onions (Scallions), sliced	100g/4 oz
Red pepper, seeded and sliced	1/1
Green pepper, seeded and sliced	1/1
Courgette (Zucchini)	1/1
Celery stalks, diced	2–3/2–3
Tomato pùree	30 ml/2 tbsp
Tomatoes, peeled, seeded and chopped	4/4
Vegetable stock	750 ml/1¼ pt
Worcester sauce	30 ml/2 tbsp
Sea salt to taste	
Freshly ground pepper to taste	
Honey	15 ml/1 tbsp
Basil, chopped	5 ml/1 tsp
Oregano, chopped	5 ml/1 tsp
Garlic cloves	2/2
Salt	5 ml/1 tsp
Tabasco (Hot pepper sauce) or 1 sliced chilli	a few drops
Pasta (for soups) or vermicelli	200g/7oz

Heat the butter or margarine

in a pan and sauté the spring onions until translucent. Add the peppers, sliced courgette and celery. Sauté briefly. Stir in the tomato purée, and tomatoes.

Pour in the stock and Worcester sauce, then season with salt, pepper, sugar, chopped herbs and the garlic crushed with salt.

Cover and leave to simmer over a medium heat for 15 minutes.

Season to taste, add a few drops of Tabasco, add the boiled pasta to the soup and serve.

Peking Soup

Ingredients

Ingredients	Metric/Imperial
Sesame oil	45 ml/3 tbsp
Spring onions (Scallions), sliced	100g/4oz
Red pepper, seeded and sliced	1/1
Carrot, sliced	1/1
Celeriac, sliced	1/2/1/2
Soya bean sprouts	150g/5oz
Chinese mushrooms, soaked	100g/4oz
Garlic cloves	2/2
Sea salt	5 ml/1 tsp
Soya sauce	30 ml/2 tbsp
Cider vinegar	30 ml/2 tbsp
Honey	30 ml/2 tbsp
Vegetable stock	750 ml/1 1/4 pt
Dry sherry	100 ml/4 fl oz
Wild rice and/or brown rice, boiled	200g/7oz

Sea salt to taste
Freshly ground pepper to taste
Chives, snipped 30 ml/2 tbsp
Egg, hard-boiled (hard-cooked)   1/1

Heat the oil in a pan, then fry vegetables until brown. Add the bean sprouts and the finely sliced mushrooms and sauté briefly. Crush the garlic with the salt, add to the vegetables, then season with

soya sauce, vinegar and honey.

Pour in the stock, cover and leave to boil over a medium heat for 8–10 minutes.

Flavour with sherry, then add the rice to the soup. Season to taste with salt and pepper.

Transfer the soup to a terrine or several individual bowls and serve sprinkled with chives and chopped egg.

• • • • • • • • • • • •

Tip

If possible, use fresh bean sprouts. You can buy them or grow them yourself from dried soya beans.

• • • • • • • • • • • •

19

Love Apple Soup

Ingredients   Metric/Imperial

For the soup:

Ripe tomatoes peeled, seeded and chopped	600g/1½lb
Butter or margarine	30ml/2 tbsp
Onion, chopped	1 large/1 large
Tomato purée	30ml/2 tbsp
Wholewheat flour	15ml/1 tbsp
Vegetable stock	600ml/1pt
Crème fraîche	225g/8oz
Sea salt to taste	
Freshly ground pepper to taste	
Mint, chopped	30ml/2 tbsp

For the semolina dumplings:

Butter	60g/2½oz
Egg, beaten	1/1
Semolina	100g/4oz
Sea salt to taste	
Freshly ground white pepper to taste	
Oil	

Additionally:

Chives, snipped	30ml/2 tbsp

Heat the butter or margarine and sauté the onion until translucent. Add the tomatoes, stir in the tomato purée, sprinkle with flour, then pour in the stock, stirring constantly. Leave to simmer over medium heat for 10–15 minutes. Cool slightly then press the soup through a fine sieve or purée in a food processor.

Reheat in a pan, stir in the crème fraîche, season with salt, pepper and mint.

To make the dumplings, cream the butter, add the beaten egg and blend in the semolina. Season with salt and pepper and leave,

covered, for about 10 minutes.

With a teaspoon, make even-shaped dumplings from the mixture. Place on to an oiled plate and leave in the

fridge for a further 20 minutes.

Simmer carefully in boiling salted water for 10 minutes.

Pour the tomato soup in to a terrine and gently transfer the dumplings from the water to the soup, draining them well. Sprinkle with chives and serve immediately.

• • • • • • • • • • • • •

Tip

You can use these semolina dumplings in any other vegetable soup.

• • • • • • • • • • • • •

Orange and Vegetable Soup

Ingredients	Metric/Imperial
Sesame oil	30ml/2 tbsp
Onion, chopped	1/1
Leek, sliced	1 small/1 small
Carrots, sliced	2/2
Red pepper, seeded and sliced	1/1
Green pepper, seeded and sliced	1/1
Chinese leaves	1 small head/ 1 small head
Oranges	2/2
Grapefruit	2/2
Vegetable stock	1 l/1¾pt
Sea salt to taste	
Freshly ground pepper to taste	
Nutmeg	a pinch/a pinch
Ground ginger	a pinch/a pinch
Caraway seeds	5ml/1 tsp
Honey	2½ml/½ tsp
Parsley, chopped	15ml/1 tbsp
Chives, snipped	15ml/1 tbsp

Heat the oil in a pan and sauté the onion until translucent.

Add the leek, carrots, and peppers to the onion. Fry gently.

Quarter the Chinese leaves, remove the stem and cut into fine strips. Add to the vegetables and gently fry for a short while.

Peel the oranges and grapefruit, then separate into segments. Add to the vegetables, and pour the stock on top.

Season with salt, pepper, nutmeg, ginger, caraway and honey. Simmer over a medium heat for 15 minutes.

Season to taste and serve sprinkled with herbs.

Chinese Egg and Mushroom Soup

Ingredients	Metric/Imperial
Sesame oil	30ml/2 tbsp
Onion, sliced	1/1
Carrot, sliced	1/1
Leek, sliced	1 small/1 small
Chinese mushrooms, soaked and sliced	100g/4oz
Vegetable stock	750ml/1¼ pt
Soya sauce	30ml/2 tbsp
Ground ginger	a pinch/a pinch
Sea salt to taste	
Freshly ground pepper to taste	
Sugar	a pinch/a pinch
Sherry	100ml/4fl oz
Egg whites	4/4
Egg yolks	4/4
Chives, snipped	30ml/2 tbsp

Heat the oil and sauté the onion until translucent.

Add the carrots, leeks and mushrooms. Sauté briefly.

Pour in the stock, season with soya sauce, ginger, salt, pepper and sugar and simmer, covered, for 5 minutes.

Stir in the sherry. Whisk the egg whites and pour through a strainer into the soup. Simmer for a further 5 minutes.

Transfer the soup in to four individual bowls. Garnish each with an egg yolk and sprinkle with chives.

22

Mimi's Lettuce Soup

Ingredients	Metric/Imperial
Butter or margarine	*30ml/2 tbsp*
Onion, chopped	*1 medium/ 1 medium*
Lettuce	*1/1*
Vegetable stock	*750ml/1¼pt*
Sea salt to taste	
Freshly ground pepper to taste	
Nutmeg	*a pinch/a pinch*
Single cream (light cream)	*100ml/4fl oz*

Additionally:

Vinegar	*15ml/1 tbsp*
Water	*½l/18fl oz*
Eggs	*4/4*
Chervil, chopped	*30ml/2 tbsp*

Heat the butter or margarine in a pan and gently fry the onion. Add the washed and torn up lettuce leaves.

Pour in the stock and cook for 15 minutes. Cool slightly. Purée in a food processor.

Reheat in a pan, season to taste with salt, pepper and nutmeg and add the cream.

Bring the vinegar and water to the boil. Poach the eggs then drain well.

Transfer the soup to individual bowls, add an egg to each and serve sprinkled with chervil.

Pepperoni Aux Herbes de Provence

Ingredients	Metric/Imperial
Peppers	4 medium/4 medium
Onions, chopped	2/2
Mushrooms, chopped	225g/8oz
Eggs, beaten	2–3/2–3
Grated Emmental cheese	100g/4oz
Breadcrumbs	30–45ml/2–3 tbsp
Parsley, chopped	30ml/2 tbsp
Sea salt to taste	
Freshly ground pepper to taste	
Nutmeg	a pinch/a pinch

Additionally:

Tomatoes, peeled, seeded and chopped	4/4
Crème fraîche	225g/8oz
White wine	225ml/8fl oz
Herbes de Provence (Basil; Rosemary — garlic as preferred)	15ml/1 tbsp

Cut a lid off each pepper, remove the seeds then wash the peppers and drain well.

Combine the eggs, onions, mushrooms, Emmental and breadcrumbs. Add the herbs then season with salt, pepper and nutmeg. Fill the peppers with this mixture and place them close together in an oven-proof dish.

Combine the tomatoes, crème fraîche and wine. Season with herbs then pour over and around the peppers.

Bake for 20 minutes in an oven preheated to 200°C/400°F/Gas 6. Serve immediately.

- - - - - - - - - - - - - - - -

Tip

You can also stuff tomatoes, Spanish onions or aubergines in this way.

- - - - - - - - - - - - - - - -

26

Soya Risotto

Ingredients	Metric/Imperial
Butter or margarine	50g/2oz
Onion, chopped	1/1
Carrots, diced	2/2
Celeriac, diced	½/½
Leek, sliced	1 small/1 small
Courgette (zucchini) diced	1/1
White wine	225ml/8fl oz
Lemon	1/1
Worcester sauce	a few dashes/ a few dashes
Soya sausages (made with soya grits and eggs)	8 small/8 small
Brown rice	250g/9oz
Vegetable stock	1 l/1¾pt
Sea salt to taste	
Freshly ground pepper to taste	
Tomatoes, peeled, seeded and chopped	4/4
Crème fraîche	225g/8oz
Chives, snipped	30ml/2 tbsp

Heat the butter or margarine in a pan and sauté the vegetables until translucent. Pour in the wine, then season with lemon juice and Worcester sauce. Cover and simmer for 5 minutes.

Add the sliced sausages and the rice and sauté briefly.

Pour in two cups of stock and leave to boil over medium heat, uncovered.

Stir occasionally, gradually adding the remaining stock. The risotto will be ready in approximately 30–40 minutes.

Season with salt and pepper and add the tomatoes and crème fraîche. Serve sprinkled with chives.

Tip

You can prepare the risotto without the sausages and serve them separately.

Spinach and Herb Loaf

Ingredients — Metric/Imperial

Ingredient	Metric/Imperial
Butter or margarine	30ml/2 tbsp
Onion, chopped	1 medium/1 medium
Spinach, fresh or frozen	500g/1lb
Bread rolls	8/8
Vegetable stock	300ml/10fl oz
Parsley, chopped	15ml/1 tbsp
Chives, snipped	15ml/1 tbsp
Chervil chopped	15ml/1 tbsp
Tarragon, chopped	15ml/1 tbsp
Garlic cloves	2/2
Sea salt	5ml/1 tsp
Crème fraîche	225g/8oz
Eggs, beaten	4/4
Wholewheat flour	30–45ml/2–3 tbsp
Breadcrumbs	30–45ml/2–3 tbsp
Oil for greasing	

Heat the butter or margarine and gently fry the onion until translucent. Wash the spinach, if it is fresh or defrost if it is frozen. Add to the onion and sauté briefly.

Crumble the rolls into the stock. Crush the garlic with salt.

Add the spinach, herbs and garlic to the stock. Fold in the crème fraîche, eggs, flour and breadcrumbs. Knead well to make a compact mixture.

Grease an oven-proof dish, transfer the spinach loaf into it, then bake for 40–45 minutes in an oven preheated to 220°C/425°F/Gas 7.

• • • • • • • • • • • • • • •

Tip

You can serve a tomato or cheese sauce with this 'roast'.

• • • • • • • • • • • • • • •

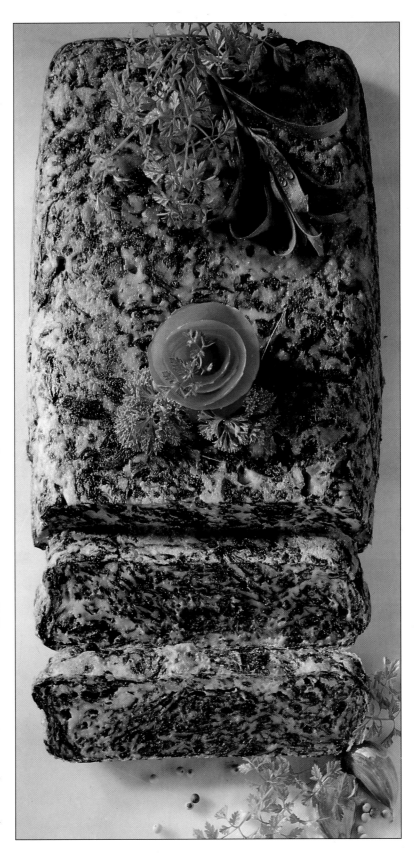

Pancakes 'Four Season'

Ingredients — Metric/Imperial

For the batter:

Wholewheat flour	100g/4oz
Milk	225ml/8fl oz
Eggs, beaten	4/4
Salt	a pinch/a pinch
Olive oil	15ml/1 tbsp

Additionally:

Mushrooms, halved	125g/4½oz
Tomatoes, peeled, seeded and chopped	2/2
Cucumber	1 small/1 small
Sweetcorn (Corn kernels)	100g/4oz
Peas	100g/4oz
Sea salt to taste	
Freshly ground pepper to taste	
Oregano, chopped	15ml/1 tbsp
Mozzarella cheese, diced	125g/4½oz
Oil for frying	
Chives, snipped	30ml/2 tbsp

Whisk the flour with the milk, eggs, salt and oil to make a smooth batter, then leave to stand.

Peel, halve, seed and slice the cucumber.

Drain the sweetcorn. Blanch the peas for 5 minutes in salted water. Drain then combine all the vegetables. Season with salt, pepper and oregano.

For each serving, pour a quarter of the batter into a frying pan, bake, then cover with a quarter of the vegetables. Transfer to an oven-proof dish. Repeat with the remaining batter and vegetables.

Sprinkle the pancakes with Mozzarella, then bake in an oven preheated to 220°C/425°F/Gas 7 for 5–10 minutes.

Remove from the oven, sprinkle with chives and serve immediately.

Stuffed Aubergines

Ingredients Metric/Imperial

Ingredients	Metric/Imperial
Aubergines (Eggplants)	2 large/2 large
Olive oil	45ml/3 tbsp
Garlic cloves	2/2
Sea salt	5ml/1 tsp
Onion, chopped	1/1
Tomatoes, peeled, seeded and chopped	4/4
Vegetable stock	225ml/8fl oz

For the stuffing:

Soya granules	225g/8oz
Low-fat quark	150g/5oz
Tomato purée	30ml/2 tbsp
Basil, chopped	5ml/1 tsp
Oregano, chopped	5 ml/1 tsp
Eggs, beaten	2/2
Chives, snipped	15ml/1 tbsp
Parsley, chopped	15ml/1 tbsp
Grated Emmenthal cheese	125g/4 1/2oz
Salt to taste	
Freshly ground pepper to taste	

Halve the aubergines and parboil for 5 minutes in salted water. Drain well.

Crush the garlic with the salt. Sauté in hot oil with the onion. Add the tomatoes and the stock, cover, and simmer for 5 minutes.

Prepare the soya granules according to the instructions on the package. Add the quark, tomato purée, spices, eggs and herbs. Mix well. If necessary, bind the mixture with some breadcrumbs.

Add the Emmenthal, season with salt and pepper and leave for 20 minutes.

Fill the aubergines with this mixture and then place in an oven-proof dish. Pour over the tomato sauce and bake in an oven preheated to 200°C/400°F/Gas 6 for 15–20 minutes. Serve immediately.

● ● ● ● ● ● ● ● ● ● ● ● ● ● ● ●

Tip

You can use this stuffing for other kinds of vegetables, for instance courgettes, cucumbers or small pumpkins.

● ● ● ● ● ● ● ● ● ● ● ● ● ● ● ●

Soya Dumplings in Beer Sauce

Ingredients	Metric/Imperial
Soya granules	225g/8oz
Vegetable stock	400ml/14fl oz
Low-fat quark	150g/5oz
Eggs, beaten	2/2
Peanut oil	30ml/2 tbsp
Mustard	15ml/1 tbsp
Marjoram, chopped	5ml/1 tsp
Garlic clove, chopped	1/1
Whisky	30ml/2 tbsp
Parsley, chopped	30ml/2 tbsp
Sea salt to taste	
Freshly ground pepper to taste	
Oil for deep-frying	

For the sauce:

Onion, chopped	1/1
Leek	1 small/1 small
Carrots	2/2
Celeriac	$^1/_2$/$^1/_2$
Olive oil	15ml/1 tbsp
Tomato purée	30ml/2 tbsp
Wholewheat flour	45ml/3 tbsp
Vegetable stock	300ml/10fl oz
Beer (flat and strong)	150ml/5fl oz
Honey	30ml/2 tbsp
Cider vinegar	30ml/2 tbsp
Marjoram	5ml/1 tbsp
Thyme	5ml/1 tbsp

Combine the soya granules with the stock. Add the quark, eggs, oil, mustard, marjoram, garlic, whisky and chopped parsley. Stir until smooth. If necessary, bind with breadcrumbs or flour. Season with salt and pepper.

Shape into little dumplings and deep-fry in hot oil. Drain well and keep warm.

To make the sauce, wash the vegetables and cut into thin strips. Heat the oil in a pan and sauté the vegetables until translucent. Stir in the tomato purée, dust with flour and pour in the stock and beer. Add the honey, vinegar, marjoram, thyme, salt and pepper. Simmer, covered, for 8–10 minutes.

Arrange the dumplings on serving dishes and pour the sauce on top. Serve immediately.

Vegetableburger

Ingredients	Metric/Imperial
Wholewheat rolls	4/4
Tartare sauce	60ml/4 tbsp
Lettuce leaves	
Radicchio leaves	
Tomato	1 large/1 large
Tofu, sliced	100g/4oz
Flour	
Egg, beaten	1/1
Golden breadcrumbs	50g/2oz
Oil for frying	
Spanish onion, sliced	1/1
Cress	1 box/1 box
Crème fraîche	50g/2oz
Mustard	30ml/2 tbsp
Sea salt to taste	
Freshly ground pepper to taste	
Soya sauce	15ml/1 tbsp
Sugar	2½ml/½ tsp

Halve the rolls and toast under the grill (broiler). Cover with tartare sauce, lettuce and radicchio leaves and sliced tomato.

Coat the tofu slices with flour, then dip in egg and breadcrumbs. Shallow fry on both sides until golden brown. Drain well. Place on top of the tomato. Garnish with onion and sprinkle with cress.

Combine the créme fraîche with the mustard, salt, pepper, soya sauce, and sugar. Spread over the burgers.

Cover with the other half of the roll before serving.

Tofu Ragout

Ingredients	Metric/Imperial
Tofu-Cauldron	250g/9oz
Vegetable stock	½l/18fl oz
Wholewheat flour	125g/5oz
Oil for frying	

Additionally:

Butter or margarine	30ml/2 tbsp
Onion, chopped	1/1
Green pepper, seeded and diced	1/1
Mushrooms, sliced	100g/4oz
White wine	225ml/8fl oz
Vegetable stock	225ml/8fl oz
Crème fraîche	100g/4oz
Cornflour (Cornstarch)	15ml/1 tbsp
Water	30ml/2 tbsp
Sea salt to taste	
Freshly ground pepper to taste	
Nutmeg	a pinch/a pinch
Soya sauce	a few dashes/a few dashes

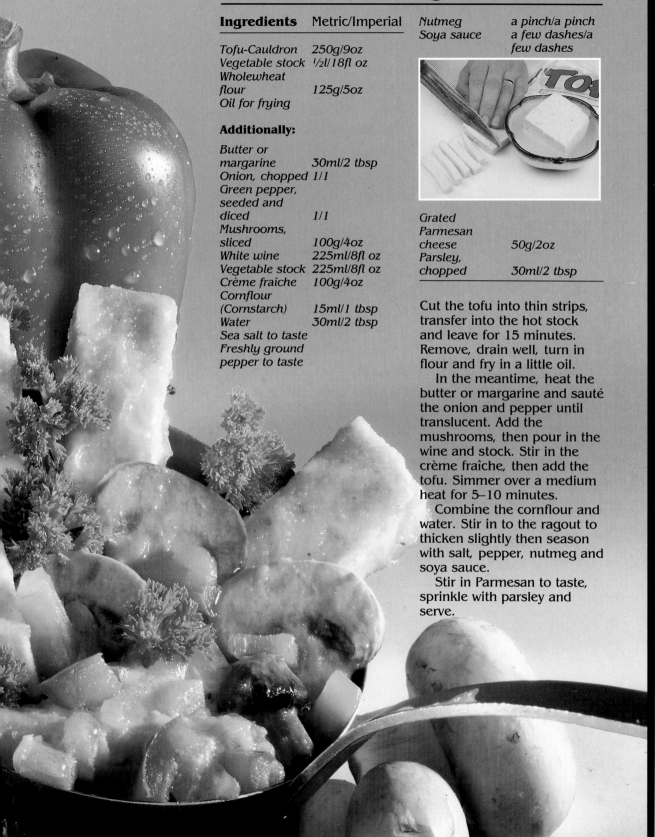

Grated Parmesan cheese	50g/2oz
Parsley, chopped	30ml/2 tbsp

Cut the tofu into thin strips, transfer into the hot stock and leave for 15 minutes. Remove, drain well, turn in flour and fry in a little oil.

In the meantime, heat the butter or margarine and sauté the onion and pepper until translucent. Add the mushrooms, then pour in the wine and stock. Stir in the crème fraîche, then add the tofu. Simmer over a medium heat for 5–10 minutes.

Combine the cornflour and water. Stir in to the ragout to thicken slightly then season with salt, pepper, nutmeg and soya sauce.

Stir in Parmesan to taste, sprinkle with parsley and serve.

33

Hearty Country Hot Pot

Ingredients

	Metric/Imperial
Soya cubes (dried)	150g/5oz
Vegetable stock	½l/18fl oz
Butter or margarine	60ml/4 tbsp
Onion, chopped	1/1
Leek, sliced	1/1
Carrots, cubed	2/2
Potatoes, cubed	4 large/4 large
Tomato purée	30ml/2 tbsp
Wholewheat flour	45ml/3 tbsp
Red wine	225ml/8fl oz
Marjoram, chopped	5ml/1 tsp
Thyme, chopped	5ml/1 tsp
Mushrooms	300g/10oz
Single cream (Light cream)	225ml/8fl oz
Blue cheese, crumbled	100g/4oz
Salt to taste	
Freshly ground pepper to taste	
Parsley, chopped	30ml/2 tbsp

Place the soya cubes into a bowl, pour the stock on top and leave for 30 minutes.

Heat the butter or margarine and gently fry the well-drained soya cubes. Add the vegetables and sauté briefly. Stir in the tomato purée, dust with flour then add the wine and the stock used for soaking the soya cubes. Season with marjoram and thyme and add the mushrooms. Simmer over a medium heat for 25–30 minutes.

Add the cream and the crumbled blue cheese, then season to taste with salt and pepper. Sprinkle with parsley and serve.

Hungarian Soya Goulash

Ingredients	Metric/Imperial
Soya cubes (dried)	150g/5oz
Vegetable stock	½l/18fl oz
Red wine	225ml/8fl oz
Olive oil	45ml/3 tbsp
Mushrooms, sliced	250g/9oz
Spanish onions, sliced	2/2
Red pepper, seeded and sliced	1/1
Green pepper, seeded and sliced	1/1
Tomato purée	30ml/2 tbsp
Wholewheat flour	30ml/2 tbsp
Tomatoes, peeled, seeded and chopped	2 large/2 large
Grated rind of lemon	15ml/1 tbsp
Sea salt	5ml/1 tsp
Garlic cloves	2/2
Ground caraway	5ml/1 tsp
Marjoram, chopped	15ml/1 tbsp
Paprika	5ml/1 tsp
Sea salt to taste	
Freshly ground pepper to taste	
Soured cream	225ml/8oz
Chives, snipped	30ml/2 tbsp

Cover the soya cubes with stock and wine and leave to soak for at least 30 minutes.

Heat the oil in a pan and briefly sauté the well-drained cubes. Add the onions, mushrooms and peppers.

Stir in the tomato purée, dust with flour, then add the tomatoes and the liquid from soaking the cubes.

Crush the garlic with salt. Add to the goulash along with the lemon rind, caraway, marjoram and paprika. Simmer over a medium heat for 25–30 minutes.

Season to taste with salt and pepper. Simmer for a further 5 minutes.

Transfer the goulash on to individual plates, garnish with a tablespoonful of cream each and sprinkle with chives.

Asparagus in White Wine Sauce

Ingredients	Metric/Imperial
Fresh asparagus	1½kg/3lb
Lemon	1/1
White wine	225ml/8fl oz
Water	½l/18fl oz
Salt	a pinch/a pinch
Butter	5ml/1 tsp

For the egg sauce:

Butter	125g/4½oz
Egg yolks	4/4
White wine	50ml/2fl oz
Lemon	1/1
Sea salt to taste	
Freshly ground pepper to taste	
Sugar	2½ml/½ tsp
Worcester sauce a dash/a dash	
Chervil, snipped 30ml/2 tbsp	

Peel the asparagus, cut to equal lengths and tie together in bundles.

Bring the lemon juice, wine, water, salt and butter to the boil. Add the bundles of asparagus and cook for 15 minutes or until tender.

In the meantime, heat the butter in a pan.

Whisk the egg yolks with the wine and lemon juice in a different pan. Season with salt, pepper, sugar and Worcester sauce. Whisk in a double boiler until the mixture becomes creamy. Fold in the warm butter, drop by drop. Season the sauce to taste, then fold in the chervil.

Arrange the asparagus on a plate, pour over the sauce and serve immediately.

Tip

This light egg sauce also goes well with any other tender vegetables.

Amsterdam Egg Bake

Ingredients	Metric/Imperial
Butter or margarine	30ml/2 tbsp
Onion, chopped	1/1
Spring onions (Scallions)	100g/4oz
Mushrooms, sliced	8–10/8–10
Fresh peaches	2/2
Tomatoes, peeled, seeded and sliced	4/4
Soured cream	225g/8oz
Grated Gouda cheese	150g/5oz
Sea salt to taste	
Freshly ground pepper to taste	
Nutmeg	a pinch/a pinch
Chives, snipped	30ml/2 tbsp

Additionally:

Hard-boiled eggs (Hard-cooked eggs)	6/6
Oil for greasing	

Heat the butter or margarine and gently fry the onion until translucent. Add the sliced spring onions and

mushrooms and sauté briefly. Plunge the peaches into boiling water for 1 minute then remove and peel. Cut in half and remove the stone. Slice the fruit.

Combine the soured cream, Gouda, salt, pepper, nutmeg and chives.

Arrange the tomatoes, peaches and sautéed vegetables in layers in a greased oven-proof dish.

Place the peeled and sliced eggs on top. Pour over the sauce.

Bake for 10–15 minutes in an oven preheated to 200°C/400°F/Gas 6.

Vegetable Croquettes

Ingredients	Metric/Imperial
Butter or margarine	30ml/2 tbsp
Onion	1/1
Cooked peas	500g/1lb
Eggs, beaten	2/2
Mustard	15ml/1 tbsp
Rolls, soaked in water	2/2
Sea salt to taste	
Freshly ground pepper to taste	
Nutmeg	a pinch/a pinch
Soya sauce	15ml/1 tbsp
Parsley, chopped	30ml/2 tbsp
Green peppercorns	5ml/1 tsp
Rolled oats, for binding	30–45ml/2–3 tbsp

Swabian Lentils

Ingredients	Metric/Imperial
Lentils, soaked overnight	400g/14oz
Vegetable stock	1/2l/18fl oz
Butter or margarine	30ml/2 tbsp
Onion, chopped	1/1
Carrots, diced	2/2
Leek, sliced	1 small/1 small
Tomato purée	30ml/2 tbsp
White wine	225ml/8fl oz
Lemon	1/1
Crème fraîche	225g/8oz
Wholewheat flour	15–30ml/1–2 tbsp
Sea salt to taste	
Freshly ground pepper to taste	
Honey	30ml/2 tbsp
Cider vinegar	60ml/4 tbsp

Additionally:

Small pasta	200g/7oz
Oil for frying	
Nutmeg	a pinch/a pinch
Chives, snipped	30ml/2 tbsp

Rinse the lentils, then boil for 15–20 minutes in the stock.

In the meantime, heat the butter or margarine and gently fry the vegetables until translucent. Stir in the tomato purée, pour in the wine and lemon juice and add to the lentils. Combine the crème fraîche with the flour and stir into the lentils. Season to taste with salt, pepper, honey and vinegar.

Cook the pasta until tender, then fry with a little fat and season with salt, pepper and nutmeg.

Arrange on a plate, spread the lentils on top and garnish with chives.

Additionally:

Wholewheat flour	150g/5 oz
Eggs, beaten	2/2
Golden breadcrumbs	150g/5oz
Oil for frying	

Heat the butter or margarine and fry the onion until golden brown.

Purée the peas in a food processor or with a mixer.

Combine the onion, mashed peas, eggs, mustard and the well-squeezed rolls to make a compact mixture. Season to taste with salt, pepper, nutmeg and soya sauce.

Knead in the parsley and peppercorns. Bind with oats.

Shape the rissoles with your hands first dipped into water. Turn first in flour, then dip in eggs and breadcrumbs.

Fry in a little oil until golden brown, drain well and serve immediately.

Tip

You can also prepare these rissoles with chick peas, beans or lentils.

39

Home-made Wholewheat Pasta

Ingredients	Metric/Imperial
Freshly ground wholewheat flour	225g/8oz
Sea salt	a pinch/a pinch
Nutmeg	a pinch/a pinch
Eggs, beaten	2/2
Olive oil	15–30ml/1–2 tbsp
Water, if necessary	15–30ml/1–2 tbsp

Place the very finely ground flour in a bowl and mix with the salt and nutmeg. Combine with the eggs, oil and, if necessary, water to make a smooth dough. Cover with a moist cloth and leave for 30 minutes.

Roll out the dough very thinly and cut into the required shape. Boil the pasta in salted water for 5–10 minutes, according to size and shape.

. . . .
Tip

You can colour the pasta by adding tomato purée, finely chopped herbs, saffron or mashed spinach to the dough.
. . . .

Mushroom Sauce

Ingredients	Metric/Imperial
Butter or margarine	45ml/3 tbsp
Onions, chopped	2 small/2 small
Chanterelles, sliced	200g/7oz
Mushrooms, sliced	400g/14oz
Flour	30ml/2 tbsp
White wine	225ml/8fl oz
Vegetable stock	400ml/14fl oz
Sea salt	
Freshly ground pepper	
Single cream (Light cream)	225ml/8fl oz
Parsley, chopped	15ml/1 tbsp
Chives, snipped	15ml/1 tbsp
Chervil, chopped	15ml/1 tbsp

Heat the butter or margarine and sauté the onions until translucent. Add the chanterelles and mushrooms to the onions. Sauté briefly. Dust with flour then pour in the wine and stock. Simmer over medium heat for 8–10 minutes.

Season with salt and pepper. Add the cream.

Fold in the herbs, adjust the seasoning and serve.

Japanese Tofu Sauce

Ingredients	Metric/Imperial
Butter or margarine	30ml/2 tbsp
Tofu, diced	150g/5oz
Onion, chopped	1/1
Red pepper, seeded and diced	1/1
Green pepper, seeded and diced	1/1
Wholewheat flour	30ml/2 tbsp
Tomatoes, peeled, seeded and chopped	2/2
Gherkins, diced	2/2
Red wine	225ml/8fl oz
Vegetable stock	225ml/8fl oz
Salt to taste	
Freshly ground pepper to taste	
Paprika	5ml/1 tsp
Curry powder	2½ml/½ tsp
Crème fraîche	100g/4oz
Chives, snipped	30ml/2 tbsp

Heat the butter or margarine and briefly fry the tofu. Add the onion and diced peppers and sauté. Dust with flour, then add the tomatoes and gherkins. Pour in the wine and stock, cover and simmer over a medium heat for 10 minutes.

Season to taste with salt, pepper, paprika and curry powder.

. . . .

Stir in the crème fraîche, pour the sauce over the cooked pasta and sprinkle with chives before serving.

. . . .

40

Leek & Cheese Roly-Poly

Ingredients   Metric/Imperial

Freshly ground wholewheat flour	200g/7oz
Egg	1/1
Oil	15ml/1 tbsp
Lukewarm water	225ml/8fl oz
Sea salt	5ml/1 tsp
Ground caraway	5ml/1 tsp
Ground coriander	2¹/₂ml/¹/₂ tsp
Honey	2¹/₂ml/¹/₂ tsp
Cider vinegar	30ml/2 tbsp

For the stuffing:

Butter or margarine	50g/2oz
Onions, chopped	2/2
Leeks, sliced	2/2
Garlic cloves	2/2
Salt	5ml/1 tsp
Low-fat quark or cream cheese	225ml/8oz
Eggs	2/2
Grated Emmenthal cheese	125g/4¹/₂oz
Breadcrumbs	30–45ml/2–3 tbsp
Sea salt to taste	
Freshly ground pepper	
Nutmeg	a pinch/a pinch
Chives, snipped	30ml/2 tbsp

Additionally:

Oil for greasing	
Egg yolk	1/1

Pour the flour on to a large worktop. Make a well in the centre and add the eggs, oil, water and honey. Sprinkle over the salt, caraway, coriander and vinegar. Mix well and knead to make a smooth dough. Cover with a moist cloth and leave for 30 minutes.

In the meantime, to prepare the stuffing, heat the butter or margarine, add the onions and leeks and sauté until translucent. Crush the garlic with salt. Add to the pan, fry briefly, then remove the pan from the heat and leave to cool.

Beat the quark with the eggs until smooth, then fold in the vegetables and the Emmenthal. Mix with the breadcrumbs, and season with salt, pepper, chives and nutmeg.

Roll the dough out until it is approximately ³/₄ cm/¹/₄ in thick. Spread a clean cloth over a pastry board or worktop and lift the pastry on to the cloth. Spread the quark mixture evenly over the pastry. Hold one side of the cloth with both hands and gently lift so that the pastry rolls over to form a loaf. Using the cloth, pat the roly-poly into a neat tubular shape. Carefully transfer to a greased baking sheet and ease away the cloth — do not allow the pastry to break. Bake for 35–40 minutes in an oven preheated to 200°C/400°F/Gas 6.

Shortly before the roly-poly is cooked, whisk the egg yolk with a little water and brush over the surface. Return to the oven to finish baking and serve warm.

Lasagne Al Forno

Ingredients   Metric/Imperial

For the stuffing:

Soya granules	200g/7oz
Water	400ml/14fl oz
Low-fat quark or cream cheese	225g/8oz
Eggs, beaten	2/2
Tomato purée	30ml/2 tbsp
Butter or margarine	45ml/3 tbsp
Onion, chopped	1/1
Carrot, diced	1/1
Celeriac, diced	1/2/1/2
Wholewheat flour	30ml/2 tbsp
Tomatoes, peeled, seeded and chopped	3/3
Garlic clove, chopped	1/1
Bay leaf, crumbled	1/1
Basil, chopped	15ml/1 tbsp
Sea salt to taste	
Freshly ground pepper to taste	

For the bechamel sauce:

Butter or margarine	50g/2oz
Wholewheat flour	50g/2oz
Milk	1/2l/18fl oz
Nutmeg	a pinch/a pinch
Grated Parmesan cheese	50g/2oz

Additionally:

Green lasagne or home-made pasta	350g/12oz
Oil for greasing	
Mozzarella cheese, sliced	200g/7oz

Combine the soya granules with the water, quark, eggs and tomato purée. Leave to stand for 20 minutes.

In the meantime, heat the butter or margarine and gently fry the vegetables until translucent. Dust with flour, then add the tomatoes and bring to the boil. Add the garlic, bay leaf and basil and season with salt and pepper. Remove from the heat and combine with the soya mixture.

To make the bechamel sauce, heat the butter or margarine and stir in the flour. Add the milk, stirring constantly, then season with salt, pepper and nutmeg. Cook for 10 minutes. Add the Parmesan to the sauce.

Cook the lasagne in a tray of boiling salted water for 6 minutes.

Grease an ovenproof dish, then fill with layers of soya mixture, bechamel sauce and lasagne. Start with lasagne and end with sauce.

Cover with Mozzarella, bake for 20 minutes in an oven preheated to 200°C/400°F/Gas 6 and serve.

● ● ● ● ● ● ● ● ● ● ● ● ● ●

Tip

If you prefer, omit the soya granules and combine the quark with 100g/4oz grated Emmenthal and 30ml/2 tbsp of breadcrumbs

● ● ● ● ● ● ● ● ● ● ● ● ● ●

43

Boiled Potatoes with Dips

Ingredients

Ingredients	Metric/Imperial
New potatoes	4 large/4 large
Caraway seeds	15ml/1 tbsp
Thyme	2 sprigs/2 sprigs
Rosemary	1 sprig/1 sprig
Peppercorns	a few/a few
Juniper berries	15ml/1 tbsp
Bay leaf	1/1

Wash the potatoes thoroughly, then bring to the boil with some salted water. Add the herbs and spices, cover the pan and leave to boil, according to the size of the potatoes, for 18–20 minutes.

Remove and serve the potatoes in their skins with the dips.

Yoghurt Cheese Dip with Herbs

Ingredients

Ingredients	Metric/Imperial
Yoghurt	225g/8oz
Cream cheese	225 g/8 oz
Onion, chopped	1/1
Parsley, chopped	15ml/1 tbsp
Chives, snipped	15ml/1 tbsp
Lemon balm, chopped	15ml/1 tbsp
Sea salt to taste	
Freshly ground pepper to taste	
Sugar	a pinch/a pinch
Juice of lemon	$1/2$/$1/2$

Beat the yoghurt with the cream cheese until smooth. Stir in the onion and chopped herbs. Season to taste with salt, pepper, sugar and lemon juice. Serve with the boiled potatoes.

Garlic Quark Dip

Ingredients	Metric/Imperial
Low-fat quark	225g/8oz
Crème fraîche	225g/8oz
Garlic cloves	2/2
Sea salt	5ml/1 tsp
Parsley, chopped	30ml/2 tbsp
Cress	1 bunch/1 bunch
Sea salt to taste	
Freshly ground pepper to taste	
Worcester sauce	a few drops/a few drops
Lemon juice	a little/a little

Beat the quark with the crème fraîche until smooth. Crush the garlic with the salt. Stir into the quark with the herbs. Season to taste with salt, pepper, Worcester sauce and lemon juice. Serve with the boiled potatoes.

Mixed Herbs Butter

Ingredients	Metric/Imperial
Butter	225g/8oz
Onion, chopped	1/1
Parsley, chopped	30ml/2 tbsp
Thyme, chopped	30ml/2 tbsp
Oregano, chopped	30ml/2 tbsp
Tarragon, chopped	30ml/2 tbsp
Mustard	30ml/2 tbsp
Worcester sauce	a few drops/a few drops
Lemon juice	15ml/1 tbsp
Sea salt to taste	
Freshly ground pepper to taste	

Whisk the butter in a bowl until creamy. Stir the onion, herbs and mustard in to the butter.

Season to taste with Worcester sauce, lemon juice, salt and pepper. Serve with the boiled potatoes.

Blue Cheese Dip

Ingredients	Metric/Imperial
Blue cheese	100g/4oz
Butter or margarine	50g/2oz
Cream cheese	100g/4oz
Crème fraîche	100g/4oz
Onion, chopped	1/1
Parsley, chopped	30ml/2 tbsp
Chervil, chopped	30ml/2 tbsp
Sea salt to taste	
Freshly ground pepper to taste	
Sugar	a pinch/a pinch
Brandy	50ml/2fl oz
Worcester sauce	a few drops/a few drops

Cream the blue cheese with a fork. Place in to a bowl then stir in the softened butter, cream cheese and crème fraîche. Beat until smooth. Fold in the onion and herbs. Season to taste with salt, pepper and sugar, adding some brandy and Worcester sauce. Serve with the boiled potatoes.

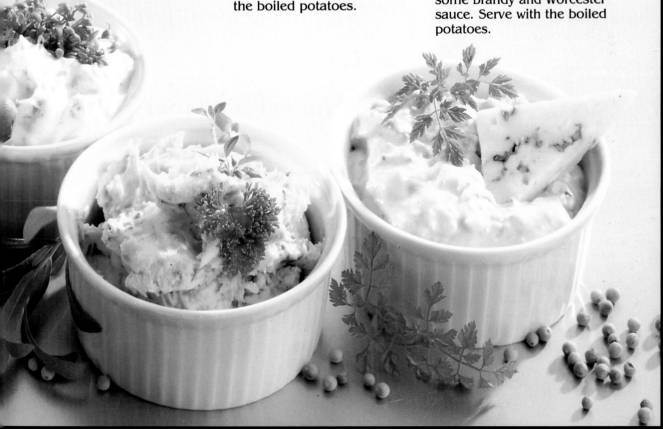

Baked Potato and Kohlrabi Mornay

Ingredients	Metric/Imperial
Potatoes	4 medium/4 medium
Kohlrabi	2 medium/2 medium
Vegetable stock	100ml/4fl oz
White wine	100ml/4fl oz
Sea salt to taste	
Freshly ground pepper to taste	

For the sauce:

Butter or margarine	40g/1½oz
Wholewheat flour	40g/1½oz
Milk	300ml/10fl oz
Single cream (Light cream)	300ml/10fl oz
Nutmeg	a pinch/a pinch
Parsley, chopped	15ml/1 tbsp
Chives, snipped	15ml/1 tbsp
Mozzarella cheese, sliced	100g/4oz

Peel the potatoes and kohlrabi, then cut them into thin strips. Spread in an oven-proof dish and pour the stock and the wine on top. Sprinkle with salt and pepper. Bake for 30 minutes in an oven preheated to 200°C/400°F/Gas 6.
In the meantime, melt the butter or margarine and stir in the flour. Pour in the milk and cream and simmer gently on a low heat for 10 minutes. Stir from time to time to prevent burning. Season the sauce with salt, pepper and nutmeg. Fold in the herbs and spread over the potatoes.
Cover with Mozzarella and brown under the grill. Serve immediately.

Potato Fritters Aix-la-Chapel

Ingredients	Metric/Imperial
Potatoes	8–10 medium/8–10 medium
Wholewheat flour	225g/8oz
Egg, beaten	1/1
Sea salt to taste	
Freshly ground pepper to taste	
Nutmeg	a pinch/a pinch
Oil for frying	

For the cabbage:

Butter	60ml/4 tbsp
Onion, chopped	1/1
White cabbage, grated	1 small/1 small
White wine	225ml/8fl oz
Vegetable stock	225ml/8fl oz
Caraway seeds	5ml/1 tsp
Cider vinegar	15–30ml/1–2 tbsp
Sugar	a pinch/a pinch
Chives, snipped	30ml/2 tbsp

Boil and peel the potatoes, then press through a sieve. Add the sieved flour and egg. Season with salt, pepper and nutmeg. Mix to make a smooth pastry. Roll into fritters 2½cm (1in) thick, and fry in hot oil until brown.
To make the cabbage, heat the butter and sauté the chopped onion until translucent. Add the grated cabbage and sauté briefly. Pour in the wine and stock, and season with caraway, vinegar and sugar. Simmer over a medium heat, covered, for 25–30 minutes.
Arrange the fritters with the cabbage on a plate and sprinkle with chives.

46

Savoury Choux Fritters

Ingredients
Metric/Imperial

Vegetable stock	250ml/9fl oz
Butter or margarine	50g/2oz
Sea salt to taste	
Freshly ground pepper to taste	
Nutmeg	a pinch/a pinch
Freshly ground wheat flour	140g/5oz
Cornflour (Cornstarch)	40g/1½oz
Wheatgerm	100g/4oz
Eggs, beaten	4–5/4–5
Parmesan cheese	125g/4½oz
Chives, snipped	30ml/2 tbsp
Oil for deep frying	

Place the stock and the butter or margarine in a pan and bring to the boil. Season with salt, pepper and nutmeg. Stir in the flour, wheat and cornflour. Continue stirring until the mixture comes off the bottom of the pan like a choux pastry.

Add the eggs a little bit at a time and then the cheese, wheatgerm and chives.

Drop spoonsful of the mixture, one at a time, into hot fat. Be sure to dip the spoon into the fat between each addition to make handling easier. When the fritters are golden, drain well. Serve either warm or cold.

• • • • • • • • • • • • •

Tip

Serve the fritters with herbed cream cheese and a fresh salad.

• • • • • • • • • • • • •

Oat Cutlet Milanese

Ingredients — Metric/Imperial

Ingredient	Metric/Imperial
Butter or margarine	30ml/2 tbsp
Onion, chopped	1/1
Leek, sliced	1 small/1 small
Vegetable stock	½ l/18fl oz
Sea salt	5ml/1 tsp
Thyme, chopped	5ml/1 tsp
Marjoram, chopped	15ml/1 tbsp
Rolled oats	160g/5½oz

Additionally:

Ingredient	Metric/Imperial
Eggs, beaten	3/3
Mustard	30ml/2 tbsp
Green peppercorns	5ml/1 tsp
Chives, snipped	30 ml/2 tbsp
Breadcrumbs for binding	30–45ml/2–3 tbsp

Olive oil for frying

For the sauce:

Ingredient	Metric/Imperial
Butter or margarine	30ml/2 tbsp
Onion, chopped	1/1
Red pepper, seeded and chopped	1/1
Sweetcorn (Corn kernels)	100g/4oz
Tomato ketchup	100ml/4fl oz
Vegetable stock	225ml/8fl oz
Crème fraîche	100g/4oz
Curry powder	5ml/1 tsp
Paprika	5ml/1 tsp
Tabasco (Hot pepper sauce)	a few drops/a few drops
Sugar	a pinch/a pinch

Heat the butter or margarine and sauté the vegetables until translucent. Pour in the stock, season with salt, thyme and marjoram and stir in the oats. Cover and simmer over a medium heat for 30 minutes.

Remove from the heat, cool, then stir in the eggs, mustard, peppercorns and chives. Bind with breadcrumbs, then shape into

cutlets. Shallow fry in olive oil until golden brown, then transfer to a serving dish and keep warm.

To make the sauce, heat the butter or margarine and sauté the onion and pepper until translucent. Add the drained sweetcorn, then the

ketchup and stock. Stir in the crème fraîche, curry powder, paprika, Tabasco or pepper sauce, salt, pepper and sugar.

Arrange the cutlets on a plate, spoon over the sauce and serve.

Buckwheat Pancakes with Cherries and Butterscotch Sauce

Ingredients	Metric/Imperial
Buckwheat flour	100g/4oz
Eggs	3/3
Sea salt	a pinch/a pinch
Milk	250ml/9fl oz
Sugar	10ml/2 tsp
Oil for frying	50ml/2fl oz

Additionally:

Butter or margarine	15–30ml/2 tbsp
Sugar	45ml/3 tbsp
Green peppercorns	15ml/1 tbsp
Red wine	450ml/16fl oz
Cherries, stoned (pitted)	200g/7oz
Ground cloves	a pinch/a pinch
Ground cinnamon	2½ ml/½ tsp
Cornflour (Cornstarch)	5ml/1 tsp
Water	75ml/5 tbsp

Beat the eggs and add the flour, salt, milk and sugar to make a smooth batter.

Heat the oil in a frying pan and pour in some batter. Cook until set, toss and cook on the second side. Keep warm on plates or a tray.

Heat the butter or margarine in a pan with the sugar until the sauce is smooth and bubbly like a butterscotch syrup, approximately 4 minutes.

Boil the stoned cherries with the wine and sugar for 2 minutes. Thicken with the combined cornflour and water. The sauce should begin to clear. Flavour with cinnamon, cloves and a few green peppercorns if you like.

Millet Cakes with Pineapple Sauerkraut

Ingredients   Metric/Imperial

Millet	150g/5oz
Vegetable stock	½l/18fl oz
Olive oil	10ml/2tsp
Onions, chopped	2/2
Sea salt to taste	
Freshly ground white pepper to taste	
Marjoram, chopped	15ml/1 tbsp
Chives, snipped	30ml/2 tbsp
Eggs, beaten	2/2
Oats for binding	30–60 ml/ 2–4 tbsp

Additionally:

Wholewheat breadcrumbs	45–60ml/ 3–4 tbsp
Oil for frying	

For the pineapple sauerkraut:

Butter or margarine	30ml/2 tbsp
Onion, chopped	1/1
Pineapple	4 slices/4 slices
Sauerkraut	500g/1lb
Vegetable stock	500ml/1pt
Green peppercorns	5ml/1 tsp
Honey	30ml/2 tbsp
Cress	1 box/1 box

Wash the millet, add to the boiling stock and simmer over a medium heat for 20 minutes.

Fry the onion in oil until golden brown and add to the millet. Season with salt, pepper and marjoram. Cool then add the chives and eggs. Bind with oats.

Using wet hands, shape little cakes out of the mixture.

Turn in the wholewheat breadcrumbs and shallow fry in hot oil until golden brown. Drain and keep warm.

To make the pineapple sauerkraut, heat the butter or margarine and gently soften the onion. Add the finely diced pineapple and the

52

sauerkraut, then pour in the stock. Season with salt, pepper and green peppercorns. Simmer, covered, for 30 minutes.

Adjust the seasoning then add the honey and finally the cress.

Arrange the millet cakes, on plates, spread sauerkraut on top and serve.

Millet Loaf Hamburg-Style

Ingredients	Metric/Imperial
Butter or margarine	30ml/2 tbsp
Onion, chopped	1/1
Leek, sliced	1/1
Red pepper, seeded and diced	1/1
Carrots, diced	2/2
Blanched peas	100g/4oz
Millet	200g/7oz
Vegetable stock	½l/18 fl oz
Parsley, chopped	30ml/2 tbsp
Lemon balm, chopped	15ml/1 tbsp
Dandelion leaves	12/12
Eggs, beaten	2/2
Grated Gouda or Cheddar cheese	100g/4oz
Sea salt to taste	
Freshly ground black pepper to taste	

Additionally:

Oil for greasing	
Mozzarella cheese, sliced	100g/4oz

Heat the butter or margarine and sauté the onion. Add the other vegetables and fry briefly. Stir in the washed millet, pour in the stock, cover and simmer for 20 minutes.

Remove from the heat, then stir in the herbs, eggs and cheese. Season with salt and pepper. Transfer to a greased ovenproof dish.

Cover with Mozzarella and bake for 15–20 minutes in an oven preheated to 200°C/400°F/Gas 6.

Mushroom Doughnuts

Ingredients   Metric/Imperial

Butter or
margarine   50g/2oz
Vegetable stock 300ml/10fl oz
Sea salt   a pinch/a pinch
Wholewheat
flour   150g/5oz
Eggs, beaten   4/4
Baking powder   2½ml/½ tsp
Frying oil

For the stuffing:

Butter   15ml/1 tbsp
Mushrooms,
sliced   250g/9oz
Herbed cream
cheese   200g/7oz
(Boursin)
White wine   100ml/4fl oz
Parsley,
chopped   15ml/1 tbsp
Tomatoes,
skinned, seeded
and chopped   2/2

Green
peppercorns in
brine   15ml/1 tbsp
Sea salt to taste
Freshly ground
pepper to taste
Caraway seeds   a pinch/a pinch
Worcester sauce 5ml/1 tsp

Put the butter, stock and salt in a pan and bring to the boil. Add the flour and stir until the mixture comes off the bottom of the pan. Remove from the heat.

Add the eggs, a little at a time, then fold in the baking powder.

Using two teaspoons, make little doughnuts from the pastry.

Deep-fry in hot oil until golden brown, then remove and keep warm.

To make the stuffing, heat the butter and sauté the mushrooms. Cool slightly, then stir in the cream cheese and the wine. Fold in the parsley, tomatoes and drained peppercorns.

Season to taste with salt, pepper, caraway seeds and Worcester sauce.

Halve the doughnuts and fill with the cheese mixture. Replace the lids and serve.

Vegetable Pizza Romana

Ingredients — Metric/Imperial

Ingredients	Metric/Imperial
Strong white flour	200g/7oz
Wholewheat flour	200g/7oz
Dried yeast	10g/1 tsp
Sugar	15ml/1 tbsp
Lukewarm water	300ml/10 fl oz
Sea salt	5ml/1 tsp
Olive oil	30ml/2 tbsp

For the topping:

Tomato purée	60ml/4 tbsp
Courgette (Zucchini), sliced	1 small/1 small
Spanish onion, sliced	1/1
Red pepper, seeded and sliced	1/1
Mushrooms sliced	100g/4oz
Tomatoes, peeled, seeded and sliced	4/4
Sea salt to taste	
Freshly ground pepper to taste	
Oregano, chopped	30ml/2 tbsp
Chives, snipped	30ml/2 tbsp
Mozzarella cheese, sliced	200g/7oz

Combine the yeast with 5ml/ 1 tsp flour and 45ml/3 tbsp tepid water. Leave for 10 minutes to activate.

Combine the flour with the yeast mixture and the sugar. Pour in the warm water, then add the salt and oil. Knead to make a smooth dough. Cover with a moist cloth and leave to rise in a warm place for 30–45 minutes.

Knead well, then roll out thinly and cover the base of four small pizza tins with the pastry.

Cover each base with 15ml/1 tbsp of tomato purée and top with courgette, onion, pepper, mushrooms and tomato slices. Sprinkle with salt, pepper, oregano and chives.

Cover with Mozzarella and transfer to an oven preheated to 200°C/400°F/Gas 6. Bake for about 20 minutes, then remove and serve.

Country Spicy Flat Bread

Ingredients	Metric/Imperial
Strong white flour	350g/12oz
Wholewheat flour	150g/5oz
Dried yeast	10g/1 tsp
Sea salt	5ml/1 tsp
Honey	15ml/1 tbsp
Milk	125ml/4fl oz
Water	125ml/4fl oz
Butter or margarine	50g/2oz
Caraway seeds	5ml/1 tsp
Coriander	5ml/1 tsp
Cardamom	5ml/1 tsp

Additionally:

Milk	60ml/4 tbsp
Sesame seeds	60ml/4 tbsp
Oil for greasing	

Combine the yeast with 5ml/ 1 tsp flour and 45ml/3 tbsp tepid water. Leave for 10 minutes to activate.

Mix the flour with the yeast mixture, salt and honey in a bowl. Add the milk, water butter or margarine and spices. Combine to make a smooth dough. Cover and leave to rise in a warm place for about 30–45 minutes.

Knead well, then shape into little flat cakes. Place on a greased baking tray. Brush with milk and sprinkle with the sesame seeds. Cover and leave to rise for 15 minutes.

Bake for 25–30 minutes in an oven preheated to 200°C/400°F/Gas 6. Remove and serve either slightly warm or cold.

Herb Rolls

Ingredients	Metric/Imperial
Freshly ground wholewheat flour	500g/1lb
Dried yeast	10g/1 tsp
Sea salt	5ml/1 tsp
Sugar	15ml/1 tbsp
Milk	225ml/8 fl oz
Butter or margarine	50g/2 oz
Egg yolks	2/2
Marjoram, chopped	15ml/1 tbsp
Thyme, chopped	5ml/1 tsp
Parsley, chopped	15ml/1 tbsp
Chives, snipped	15ml/1 tbsp

Additionally:

Egg yolks	2/2
Caraway seeds	15ml/1 tbsp
Coriander seeds	15ml/1 tbsp

Combine the yeast with 5ml/
1 tsp flour and 45ml/3 tbsp
tepid water. Leave for
10 minutes to activate.

Combine the flour with the
yeast mixture, salt and sugar.
Add the lukewarm milk,
butter and egg yolks. Add the
marjoram, thyme, parsley
and chives. Mix to make a
smooth pastry. Cover and
leave to rise in a warm place
for 30–45 minutes.

Knead thoroughly, then roll
out on a floured worktop to
about 2–3cm (¾–1¼ in) in
thickness.

Using a round shape, cut
out little rolls. Place on a
floured baking tray, cover and
leave to rise for a further
15 minutes.

Brush with egg yolk
combined with water and
sprinkle with caraway and
coriander seeds.

Bake for 15 minutes in an
oven preheated to
200°C/400°F/Gas 6 and serve
warm or cold.

Buttermilk Bread

Ingredients	Metric/Imperial
Freshly ground	
spelt	675g/1lb 7oz
Dried yeast	10g/1 tsp
Buttermilk	½ l/18fl oz
Honey	30ml/2 tbsp
Sea salt	5ml/1 tsp
Ground caraway	5ml/1 tsp
Ground	
coriander	5ml/1 tsp
Allspice	a pinch/a pinch
Oil for greasing	

Combine the yeast with 5ml/
1 tsp spelt and 45ml/3 tbsp
tepid water. Leave to activate
for 10 minutes.

Combine the spelt with the
yeast mixture. Add the
buttermilk and honey. Mix to
make a smooth dough.
Season with salt, caraway,
coriander and allspice.

Place the dough in a
greased loaf pan. Cover and
leave to rise in a warm place
for 30–45 minutes.

Bake for 45–50 minutes in
an oven preheated to
200°C/400°F/Gas 6. Remove,
leave to cool completely and
serve.

Tip

*Spelt, also called German
wheat, is a special kind of
wheat. You can replace it
with other wheat.*

57

Sweet Corncake with Strawberry Butter

Ingredients — Metric/Imperial

Ingredients	Metric/Imperial
Wholewheat flour	150g/5oz
Cornmeal (maize)	150g/5oz
Baking powder	10ml/2 tsp
Sea salt	a pinch/a pinch
Yoghurt	225g/8oz
Honey	50g/2oz
Eggs	2/2
Oil	60ml/4 tbsp

For the butter:

Strawberries	250g/9oz
Lemon	1/1
Butter	150g/5oz
Vanilla essence	6 drops/6 drops
Castor sugar (superfine sugar)	30ml/2 tbsp

Combine the flour, cornmeal, baking powder and salt in a mixing bowl. Add the yoghurt, honey, eggs and oil. Mix to make a smooth dough. Turn on to a floured worktop and roll out until the dough is approximately 1¼ cm/½ inch thick. Cut into rounds approximately 6 cm/2½ inches in diameter. Place the corncakes on a greased baking tray and bake for 10–15 minutes in an oven preheated to 200°C/400°F/ Gas 6.

In the meantime, purée the strawberries.

Add the lemon juice and vanilla essence to the butter and whisk until creamy.

Add the strawberry purée and sugar to the butter. Combine well with a whisk, then leave to cool in the fridge.

Serve the corncakes with the strawberry butter.

Sweetcorn Balls

Ingredients — Metric/Imperial

Ingredients	Metric/Imperial
Eggs	2/2
Honey	50g/2oz
Wholewheat flour	50g/2oz
Ground almonds	50g/2oz
Sweetcorn (Corn kernels)	250g/9oz
Oil for deep-frying	

For the sauce:

Demerara sugar	50g/2oz
Butter	30ml/2 tbsp
Red wine	500ml/18fl oz
Morello cherries, stoned	250g/9oz
Cinnamon	2½ml/½ tsp
Vanilla essence	6 drops/6 drops
Icing sugar (Confectioners' sugar)	5ml/1 tsp

Whisk the eggs with the honey until creamy. Fold in the flour and almonds. Stir in the drained sweetcorn.

Using two teaspoons, cut off little balls from the mixture and deep-fry in hot

oil until golden brown. Remove and keep warm.

To make the sauce, caramelize the sugar and butter in a frying pan. Pour in the wine, then add the cherries and bring to the boil once.

Season with cinnamon and vanilla essence and bind with some icing sugar.

Serve the sweetcorn balls with the sauce.

58

Yoghurt Torte with Fruits

Ingredients — Metric/Imperial

For the pastry:

Eggs	2/2
Honey	80–100g/3–4oz
Sieved wholewheat flour	100g/4oz
Baking powder	10ml/2 tsp
Vanilla essence	6 drops/6 drops

For the filling:

Yoghurt	500g/1lb
Whipping cream	225ml/8fl oz
Honey	75g/3oz
Vanilla essence	6 drops/6 drops
Gelatine	25g/1oz
Castor (Superfine) sugar	25g/1oz

For decorating:

Fruit, according to season	100g/4oz
Melted jam	50g/2oz
Flaked almonds	100g/4oz

Whisk the eggs with the honey until fluffy. Combine the flour with the baking powder. Add to the eggs along with the vanilla essence. Make into a smooth pastry, roll out, and transfer to a greased round baking tin. Bake for about 20 minutes in an oven preheated to 200°C/400°F/Gas 6. Remove and cool.

In the meantime, put the yoghurt in a bowl.

Whisk the cream until firm. Stir the honey and vanilla essence into the yoghurt.

Combine the gelatine and sugar. Dissolve in 100ml/4fl oz boiling water and stir into the yoghurt. Cool then carefully fold in the whipped cream. Leave to set for 5 minutes, then spread on the pastry base.

Garnish with fruit and glaze with jam. Leave to set completely in the fridge, then remove from the baking tin.

Toast the flaked almonds and garnish the edge of the gateau.

- - - - - - - - - - - - - -

Tip

You can replace the yoghurt with buttermilk or Biogarde.

- - - - - - - - - - - - - -

61

Apple Sorbet with Mint

Ingredients — Metric/Imperial

Ingredients	Metric/Imperial
Slightly sour apples	4 large/4 large
White wine	225ml/8fl oz
Water	100ml/4fl oz
Honey	75ml/5 tbsp
Lemon	1/1
Mint	6 leaves/6 leaves

Peel, core and finely dice the apples. Add to the wine and water and purée with a food processor. Add the honey and

lemon juice. Transfer to a freezer-proof dish and freeze.

Occasionally stir the sorbet with a spoon while it is freezing. Just before it sets, stir in the finely chopped mint.

Before serving, whisk the ice with a handmixer and transfer to individual glasses.

Home-Made Almond Ice Cream

Ingredients — Metric/Imperial

Ingredients	Metric/Imperial
Eggs	4/4
Honey	80g/3oz
Vanilla essence	6 drops/6 drops
Whipping cream	100ml/4fl oz
Anisette liqueur	50ml/2 fl oz

Additionally:

Whipped cream	225ml/8fl oz
Butter or margarine	30ml/2 tbsp
Flaked almonds	75ml/6 tbsp

Whisk the eggs with the honey and vanilla essence until creamy. Whisk the cream until very stiff.

Combine the egg mixture, cream and Anisette liqueur. Transfer to a freezer-proof bowl and place in the freezer compartment of the fridge.

For serving, transfer to individual bowls. Decorate with a spoonful of cream.

Heat the butter or margarine in pan and toast the almonds in it. Sprinkle on top of the cream.

Index

64